DATE DUE

	OCT 27 1985	
OCT 24 1985	NOV 23 1992	
FEB 28 1986	FEB.13.1989	
MAR 15 1986		
APR 5 1986		
MAR 28 1986		
MAY 17 1988		
JAN 5 1989		
FEB 25 1990		

The Wisdom of the Dragon

The Wisdom of
the Dragon

·ASIAN PROVERBS·

·COMPILED BY·

Induk Pahk

Drawings by Gloria Kim

HARPER & ROW, PUBLISHERS
New York, Evanston, and London

To
Estelle C. Carver
who has guided many to
the Source of wisdom

A proverb is
the experience of many
and the wit of one.

.

The fear of the lord is the
beginning of wisdom.
Psalm 111:10

A small beginning can become a great ending.

There is one phoenix in a thousand chickens.

소금섬 지고
물에 뛰어들사,
화약을 안고
불에 뛰어들지

Why plunge into water with a bag of salt
or jump into fire with gunpowder?

If you want to catch a tiger,
go to a tiger's den.

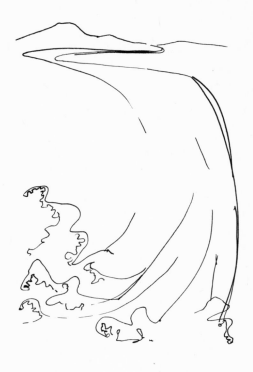

It takes a precipice to make a waterfall.

毫里之差千里之差

A hairbreadth apart makes a
thousand-mile difference.

There are times when the sun shines
even in the rathole.

Like minds get together.

The harder you beat the gong,
the louder the sound.

Do not ask for hot water at the well.

울며 겨자먹기

If you want to eat mustard, expect to cry.

One's utmost moves the heavens.

Even an ox needs a fence to rub against.

Seeing once is worth hearing a hundred times.

It's hard to get one's own sword back
when it's in someone else's scabbard.

No news is good news.

A small pepper, but hot.

배 주고 속 빌어먹기

You give away a pear and beg for its core.

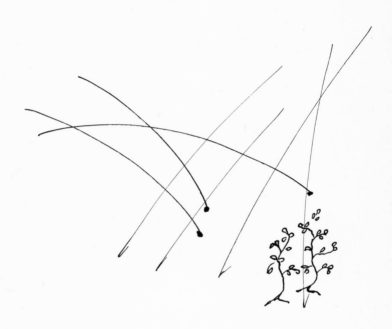

Sown soybeans, reaped soybeans.

길을 알려면
가 보아야 만 하고.
고기 맛을 알려면
씹어야 하고,
사람을 알려면
사귀어 봐야 한다

To know a road one must travel,
To know the taste of meat one must chew,
To know a person one must get acquainted.

If you play with fire, you get burned.

One cannot be a general without soldiers.

When one falls into a pit,
he either dies or rises.

떡은 둘릴수록
줄어들고,
말은 둘릴수록 는다

Cake gets smaller when passed around,
but words increase from one to another.

Whether it's short or long,
it has to be compared.

有恒產有恒心

Where your treasure is, there your heart is.

What you say is heard by mice in the night
and by birds in the day.

소인은 제 생각만 한다

One who thinks of himself is a very small man.

When you try to trap someone, you are trapped.

미운 애기 떡 한개 더 준다

Give one extra piece of cake to a stepchild.

When two hands clap, there is sound.

初不得三

If you don't win on the first try,
you may on the third.

A big mountain has a deep cavern.

멧돌 잡으러 가다가
집돌 잃는다

While one hunts a wild boar,
his own are stolen at home.

One who crawls cannot beat the runner.

남의 걱정하다가
이남박쓴다

Do not buy someone else's problems.

Why fix the barn after the ox has been stolen?

Stocked-up pantry creates hospitality.

Don't blow the bugle after the
magistrate has passed by.

애들 싸움이
어른 싸움 된다

The children's quarrel becomes their parents'.

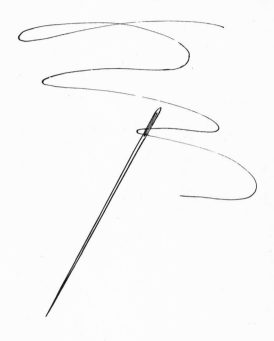

Thread follows the needle,
the needle never follows the thread.

제 아들을 알려면,
그 애 동무들을
알아봐야 한다

If you want to know your child,
find out who his friends are.

A woman who does not know how to make cake
blames the flour.

시작이 반이다

Well begun is half done.

A boat is useless without water.

도둑이 제발 저리다

One who has a guilty conscience trembles.

A crying baby gets the milk.

바늘 도적이
소 도적 된다

Stealing a needle leads to stealing an ox.

Do not worry before crossing the bridge.

금강석도 갈아야만
광채가 난다

A diamond must be cut and polished to have brilliance.

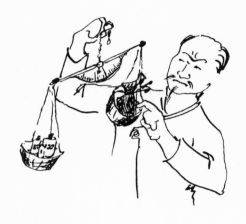

One cannot deceive a scale.

듣는 것은 잊고,

보는 것은 기억하고,

하는 것은 안다

What you hear, you forget,
What you see, you remember,
What you do, you know.

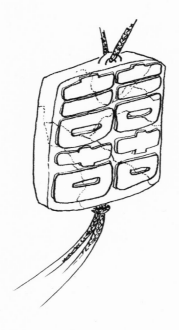

There is a flaw even in jade.

習慣第二天性

Habit becomes second nature.

If you dig a well,
keep on digging until you get water.

Why make a boil by scratching?

일 년지계는 농사에.
십년지계는 식목에
백년지계는
학교세움에 있다

If you would plan for a year, plant a crop,
If you would plan for ten years, plant a tree,
If you would plan for one hundred years, build a school.

Even a dog knows his own master.

쓸데없이
원수 맺지 말라

Do not make an enemy unnecessarily;
you may need him as a friend.

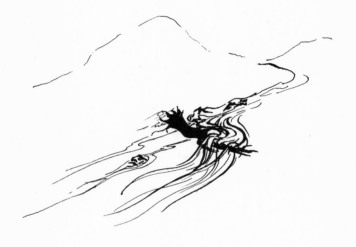

A fallen tree trunk can change the course of a stream.

백년을 못살면서,
천년 걱정하고 있다

You do not live one hundred years,
yet you worry enough for a thousand years.

Even though attacked by a tiger,
do not lose heart.

공것이 없다

Nothing comes from nothing.

A turtle travels only when he sticks his neck out.

일기와 남편의 마음은
예상치 못한다

Two unpredictables you will find,
the weather and the husband's mind.

Do not swim against the current.

돈에 날개가 돋쳤다

Money has wings.

To watch is easy, to act is difficult.

등묵 과녁가 서러워 한다

Widows sympathize with each other.

Do not kill a mosquito with a sword.

지는 해를
걷잡지 못한다

No one can stop the setting sun.

A long tail is apt to be stepped on.

잠은 죽엄의
그림자이다

Sleep is a shadow of death.

No smoke comes out of the chimney
without a fire in the stove.

Why run on a wrong road?

Even a fish wouldn't get into trouble
if it kept its mouth shut.

There are blessings in disguise.

The dog you raised bites your heel.

소금먹은 사람이
물을 켠다

One who eats a lot of salt must drink a lot of water.

Yearning for something unobtainable is like
hungering for a cake in a picture.

먼길엔 눈섭도 무겁다

On a long journey, even one's eyelids get heavy.

It's dark under the lamp.

이웃 사촌이다

A good neighbor is as good as one's own cousin.

A dog can outrun a rooster, but the rooster
can fly to the top of the roof.

If you don't put in, you don't put on.

There is no use in having even three bags of beads
unless they are strung.

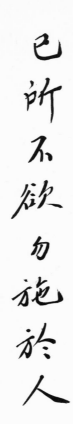

己所不欲勿施於人

What you do not like done to you,
do not unto others.

No monk can shave his own head.

When the upper stream is clear, so the lower stream.

발없는 말이
철리간다

Words have no wings, but
they fly a thousand miles.